ALBERT EINSTEIN
A Curious Mind

by Sarah Albee
pictures by Gustavo Mazali

HARPER
An Imprint of HarperCollinsPublishers

Albert Einstein asked

a lot of questions.

He was a curious kid.

But even after he grew up,

he kept on asking questions.

He never lost his sense of wonder.

Dear Parent:
Your child's love of reading starts here!

Every child learns to read in a different way and at his or her own speed. Some go back and forth between reading levels and read favorite books again and again. Others read through each level in order. You can help your young reader improve and become more confident by encouraging his or her own interests and abilities. From books your child reads with you to the first books he or she reads alone, there are I Can Read Books for every stage of reading:

SHARED READING
Basic language, word repetition, and whimsical illustrations, ideal for sharing with your emergent reader

BEGINNING READING
Short sentences, familiar words, and simple concepts for children eager to read on their own

READING WITH HELP
Engaging stories, longer sentences, and language play for developing readers

READING ALONE
Complex plots, challenging vocabulary, and high-interest topics for the independent reader

I Can Read Books have introduced children to the joy of reading since 1957. Featuring award-winning authors and illustrators and a fabulous cast of beloved characters, I Can Read Books set the standard for beginning readers.

A lifetime of discovery begins with the magical words "I Can Read!"

Visit www.icanread.com for information
on enriching your child's reading experience.

For science teachers everywhere
—S.A.

To my brother, Daniel
—G.M.

Picture credits
Copyright © Getty images: page 26: Albert and Maja Einstein as children, Bettmann; Einstein as a fourteen
year old, ullstein bild Dtl.; page 27: Einstein writing equation on the blackboard, Bettmann; Albert Einstein
is sworn in as an American citizen, New York Daily News Archive; page 28: kids on a train, Jekaterina
Nikitina; page 30: (from top to bottom) Einstein arrives in New York, Bettmann; Albert Einstein in his study,
Lucien Aigner; Einstein in a sailboat, Photo 12; page 31: Spiral galaxy and black hole, Andrzej Wojcicki/
Science Photo Library; page 32: Albert Einstein, Bettmann
Copyright © Shutterstock: page 29: train platform, Chubykin Arkady; page 31: solar panel, Kajano; elevator,
Duda Vasilii; rocket ship, iurii

Albert Einstein: A Curious Mind
Copyright © 2020 by HarperCollins Publishers

Library of Congress Control Number: 2019955935
ISBN 978-0-06-243270-4 (trade bdg.)—ISBN 978-0-06-243269-8 (pbk.)

Book design by Marisa Rother
20 21 22 LSCC 10 9 8 7 6 5 4 3 2 ❖ First Edition

Albert was born in Germany.

His father was an engineer.

His mother was a musician.

When Albert was still a baby,

they moved from a small town

to a big city.

Little Albert did not speak
until he was nearly three years old.
But his loving parents knew
their son was gifted.

When Albert was about four,
his father gave him a compass.
The compass fascinated Albert.
What invisible force
made the needle point north?

Albert began to learn the violin.

He loved it.

Music helped him think.

He played for the rest of his life.

At school, Albert was a star student
in math and science.
He was not as strong
in other subjects.
One of Albert's teachers told him
he would never amount to anything.

Albert's classes were dull.

The teachers did not want students
to ask questions.

Albert daydreamed a lot.

When Albert was about twelve,

a grown-up friend gave him a book.

It was all about geometry.

Albert read the whole thing

and solved every problem.

Soon he knew more than the friend.

At sixteen, Albert took an exam

to get into a college in Switzerland.

He scored high in math and science.

He failed the other parts.

One year later,

he took the test again and passed.

Albert kept asking questions.

He questioned rules.

(This annoyed his teachers.)

He even questioned laws—

including the laws of physics.

To rest his brain,

he played the violin.

Beautiful harmony pleased him.

It may have helped him understand

the harmony of the universe.

Albert Einstein started a family.

He wanted a teaching job,

but he couldn't find one.

And he needed money.

So he got a job in an office.

It gave him time to think.

What is light? What is energy?

When he wasn't at work,

Albert kept on thinking.

What is time?

Do atoms and molecules exist?

(Not everyone thought so.)

He had a childlike sense of wonder

at how nature worked.

Einstein did not have a laboratory
to perform his experiments.
So he pictured them in his mind.
He called them
"thought experiments."

In 1905, Einstein turned twenty-six.
He published four articles that year.
They explained many mysteries
about the universe.
They changed science forever.

Four years later,

Einstein was offered a job

at a university.

Today Einstein is best known

for his famous equation: $E = mc^2$.

The equation helps explain

his special theory of relativity.

Years later, when Einstein was forty,

his theory was confirmed

by other scientists.

That made him famous.

In the 1930s, Hitler ruled Germany.

Jewish people were not safe there.

Einstein was Jewish.

He and his family moved to the US.

Then World War II started.

Einstein hated war.

But he knew Hitler must be stopped.

Some of his ideas were used

by other scientists

to build bombs and weapons.

Albert Einstein loved kids.

He shared their joy and curiosity about the world.

He never stopped asking questions.

"Imagination is more important than knowledge," he said.

Timeline

1879
Albert Einstein is born in
Ulm, Germany, on March 14.

1880
Einstein's family moves
to Munich, Germany.

1881
Einstein's sister,
Maja, is born.

1894
Einstein's family moves
to Milan, Italy. Einstein
remains behind to
finish school.

1895
Einstein leaves Munich
and joins his family in
Switzerland. In 1900 he
graduates from university
there.

1901
Einstein becomes a
citizen of Switzerland.

1902
Einstein gets an office
job in Switzerland.

1840

1850

1860

1870

1880

1890

1900

Timeline (continued)

1905

Einstein publishes four articles that change the field of science. He also formulates the equation $E = mc^2$.

1909

Einstein gets a job as a professor of physics at a university in Switzerland.

1914

Einstein accepts a position in Germany as a professor.

1922

Einstein receives the Nobel Prize in Physics.

1930

Einstein travels to America to teach.

1933

Einstein moves to the US.

1940

Einstein becomes a US citizen.

1955

Albert Einstein dies on April 18.

Einstein's Special Theory of Relativity

Here's one way to think about this theory: If you are riding on a train sitting next to your friend, your friend does not look like she is moving *relative* to you.

But if you are standing on the train platform watching your friend on the train pass by, your friend would look like she was traveling very fast *relative* to you. Einstein's theory is that motion is "relative." The place where you are observing from is very important when describing motion.

Fun Facts about Albert Einstein

Albert Einstein had wild hair and twinkly eyes.

He wore rumpled clothes. He did not like to wear socks.

Einstein loved to sail, but he was not very good at it. His neighbors at the seashore often helped him when his sailboat fell over.

Einstein's Theories Helped Pave the Way for Future Scientists and Inventors

Although Einstein did not invent these things, we have him to thank for:

- Everyday products like paper towels, toothpaste, and dishwashing soap
- Solar power
- Movie cameras
- Lasers
- Automatic doors
- Space travel

The general theory of relativity helped later scientists predict the existence of black holes.

In Einstein's Own Words

"Life is like riding a bicycle. To keep your balance you must keep moving."

"I have no special talents. I am only passionately curious."